Useful Rh

Useful Rhetorical Devices
Ian McKenzie

Publisher – Ian McKenzie

OptimisingOutcomes with Ian

www.IansBooks.com

First Printing: 2015

ISBN: 978-1-329-09504-5

www.IansBooks.com

Contents

Page 9

Useful Rhetorical Devices

Rhetoric is the art of persuasive speaking or writing. Therefore it is very useful to use in giving presentations. Many different compositional techniques can be used in rhetoric. Combining paralinguistics with rhetorical devices can work together to make an ordinary presentation into a great presentation.

Here is an extensive list of rhetorical devices with an explanation of how they could be used. Some you may already use, some you may never use, but here they are to explore at your leisure.

Do not be too concerned about learning the names of the various rhetorical devices. The names don't really matter. What does matter is learning which of these devices may be useful to you in giving a presentation. Experiment and try them out. See which devices may suit you, your topic and your presentation style.

Of all the possible devices to use, and as you can see there are many, probably the most powerful rhetorical device used by great public speakers throughout history, is "the power of three". The number "three" has power. It has much more power than "two" or "four" or any other number. It is discussed near the end of the following list under the heading "tricolon".

Alliteration

Alliteration consists of the repetition of the same sound at the beginning of several consecutive words. It is often used in poetry and sometimes in song lyrics. I have made use of alliteration in the title of this book, "Powerful, Professional, Personal Presentations". The consonant "P" is repeated at the beginning of each word in the title. Another well-known phrase using alliteration is, "Peter Piper Picked a Peck of Pickled Peppers".

Allusion

An allusion is when something is referred to indirectly or by implication. The audience is required to make the connection. An example of an allusion is, "being a good Samaritan he assisted the injured boy across the road". This example alludes to the biblical story of the Good Samaritan. Another example could be, "she was such a liar it is surprising her nose didn't grow like Pinocchio's". In the children's story, "The Adventures of Pinocchio" written by Carlo Collodi, Pinocchio's nose would grow every time he told a lie.

Amplification

Amplification is the many ways that an explanation or a description can be expanded or enriched. Speakers or writers will often repeat something they have already said, but give more details or information. Amplification will focus the audience's or reader's attention on the main idea which is being expressed.

An example from the literature, Charles Dickens, "Our Mutual Friend" 1864-65, is given below.

"Mr. and Mrs. Veneering were bran-new people in a bran-new house in a bran-new quarter of London. Everything about the Veneerings was spic and span new. All their furniture was new, all their friends were new, all their servants were new, their place was new, . . . their harness was new, their horses were new, their pictures were new, they themselves were new, they were as newly-married as was lawfully compatible with their having a bran-new baby, and if they had set up a great-grandfather, he would have come home in matting from Pantechnicon, without a scratch upon him, French-polished to the crown of his head".

Anacoluthon

Anacoluthon is a rhetorical device which deliberately creates a break in the grammatical sequence of a sentence. It is more often used in spoken English than written English. It is used both intentionally and unintentionally.

Let's take a look at "The Walrus and the Carpenter" by Lewis Carroll

> "The time has come," the walrus said,
> "To talk of many things:
> Of shoes – and ships – and sealing wax -
> And cabbages – and – kings –
> And why the sea is boiling hot –
> And whether pigs have wings."

In the Walrus's talk to the listening oysters there is a constant interruption to his grammatical flow of the sentences.

In speeches or even casual conversation, anacoluthon is used in a way that the resulting sentence would not be considered grammatically correct. The expectation at the start of a sentence is not fulfilled.

Used deliberately in a presentation it will cause confusion with the audience and will thus make them more attentive.

The word "anacoluthon" comes from the Greek "an" meaning "not" and "akolouthos" meaning "following".

A few more examples:
"I was preparing my speech – the kettle boiled".
"I should just go and – lets discuss the next topic".

Here is an example from the classics. Hamlet's Soliloquy in Shakespeare's play "King Lear".

"To die, to sleep –
No more – and by a sleep to say we end
The heartache, and the thousand natural shocks
That flesh is heir to?
To die, to sleep –
To sleep – perchance to dream: ay, there's the rub?

Anadiplosis

Anadiplosis is a rhetorical device in which the last word or phrase of one clause or sentence is also the start of the next. This repetition draws our attention to the particular word or phrase in question. Our attention is drawn because of the pattern which has been established. Anadiplosis is sometimes referred to as "duplication". The devise is often used when building up to a climax.

Here are a few examples:

"I am Sam, Sam I am." – (Dr. Seuss, "Green Eggs and Ham")
"The general who became a slave. The slave who became a gladiator. The gladiator who defied and emperor." – The movie "Gladiator"
"Fear leads to anger. Anger leads to hate. Hate leads to suffering." Yoda in "Star Wars".
John often went to the park. The park where he would meet his friends. His friends were always there waiting. Waiting for what?
Another example of anadiplosis is directly related to the subject of this book.
"To calm the butterflies you must be relaxed. To be relaxed, you must be confident. To be confident, you must be prepared and rehearsed."
(Businessballs.com web site)

Analogy

An analogy is simply a comparison between two different things which are quite different from each other. It is a very commonly used and effective rhetorical device. Metaphors and similes are rhetorical devices discussed elsewhere in this chapter. They are related to analogies but are different from them.

She was as quiet as a mouse.
He is like a rock.
There are plenty of fish in the sea.
I feel like a fish out of water.
Bing Crosby had a velvet voice.
Life is like a box of chocolates. (Forrest Gump)
The sword may be the weapon of the warrior, but the pen is the weapon of the writer.
You are as annoying as nails across a blackboard.
Hot is to cold as fire is to ice.
This presentation is like cutting of your nose to spite your face.
This lesson is like cheering for the visiting team.

Anaphora

Anaphora is used by presenters to appeal to the audience's emotions. It is a rhetorical device used to inspire and persuade them.

Anaphora is the deliberate repetition of the first part of the sentence.

Here are some examples of anaphora:
"Every day, every night, in every way, I am getting better and better."
"Mad world! Mad kings! Mad composition." (Shakespeare)

Anastrophe

The normal structure of sentences in the English language is, subject, verb, object. In an anastrophe this order is changed. We could have for example object, subject, verb.

The word comes from the Greek language and means a turning back or about.

The use of anastrophe is common in both Greek and Latin and the devise has been used effectively by several English poets. The unusual word order draws our attention to the phrase in question.

Here are a few examples.

Yoda's speech in Star Wars.
"Powerful you have become. The dark side I sense in you."

"Death is a natural part of life. Rejoice for those around you who transform into the Force. Mourn them do not. Miss them do not. Attachment leads to jealousy. The shadow of greed, that is."

He stared into the lady's eyes, blue and beautiful.

Intelligent, he was not.

"Sure I am of this, that you have only to endure to conquer." (address delivered by Winston Churchill, 1914)

Antanaclasis

Antanaclasis uses repetition of a single word or phrase, but with a different meaning. The rhetorical devise is commonly used in jokes, and can be a useful devise to draw attention to your presentation.

Here are some examples.

"We must, indeed, all hang together, or assuredly we shall all hang separately." (Benjamin Franklin in the signing of the Declaration of Independence)

"I'm not a businessman, I'm a business man!" (song "Diamonds from Sierra Leone")

Time flies like an arrow; fruit flies like a banana.

A tagline sometimes used on social media sites, "If you like it, please 'like' it."

"If it's not on, it's not on." (Sexual health campaigns promoting the use of condoms.)

"If you aren't fired with enthusiasm, you will be fired with enthusiasm." (Vince Lombardi)

"People on the go . . . go for Coke." (Coca Cola advertisement)

Antanagoge

Antanagoge places a criticism and a compliment together to lessen the impact. Sometimes it is used to turn a negative into a positive.

Some examples.

The car is not great to look at, but it runs well.

When life gives you lemons, make lemonade.

Yes, I don't have a class this Saturday, so I won't get paid, but I am looking forward to spending time at home.

Antimetabole

Antimetabole is the repetition of words in successive clauses, but in a different order.

Examples:

"Ask not what your country can do for you; ask what you can do for your country". (John F. Kennedy in his inaugural address 1993)

If you fail to plan, you plan to fail.

"If you can't be with the one you love, love the one you're with". (Billy Preston)

Antiphrasis

In rhetoric, antiphrasis uses words or phrases contrary to their normal meaning to get an ironic or humerous effect.

Examples.

"I was awakened by the dulcet tones of Frank, the morning doorman, alternately yelling my name, ringing my doorbell, and pounding on my apartment door". (Dorothy Samuels, "Filthy Rich". William Morrow, 2001)

During the heat wave it was a cool thirty-nine degrees Celsius in the shade.

"Get in the car shorty", he told his friend who was six feet six inches tall.

Antistrophe

Antistrophe, (also called Epistrophe), involves the repetition of words at the end of successive clauses. The word also refers to an ancient dance in which dancers stepped sometimes to the right and sometimes to the left.

Examples:

Selfishness is not living as one wishes to live. It is asking others to live as one wishes to live . . . .

She is the object of my desire, just as I am the object of her desire.

"Government of the people, by the people, for the people". (Abraham Lincoln)

Antithesis

Antithesis involves the introduction of opposites in the same sentence to give a contrasting effect.

Examples:

"Never give in – never, never, never, in nothing great of small, large or petty, never give in except to convictions of honour and good sense". (Winston Churchill)

Many are called, but few are chosen.

"We must learn to live together as brothers or perish together as fools". (Martin Luthor King, Jr. 1964)

"To err is human; to forgive divine". ("An Essay on Criticism" by Alexander Pope)

Snow White and the Wiked Witch. (Snow White)

"Give every man thy ear, but few thy voice". ("Hamlet" by William Shakespeare

"That's one small step for man, one giant leap for mankind". (Neil Armstrong)

"Patience is bitter, but it has a sweet fruit". (Aristotle)

"Integrity without knowledge is weak and useless, and knowledge without integrity is dangerous and dreadful". (Samuel Johnson)

Aporia

Aporia is used as a rhetorical device in which the speaker expresses some doubt, often simulated, about his or her position and asks the audience how to proceed.

Examples:

Hamlet's soliloquy in "Hamlet" by William Shakespeare is a good example of aporia.

"To be, or not to be: that is the question.
Whether 'tis nobler in the mind to suffer
The slings and arrows of outrageous fortune,
Or to take arms against a sea of troubles,
And by opposing end them? To die: to sleep;
Than fly to others that we know not of?
Thus conscious does make cowards of us all . . ."

Aposiopesis

Aposiopesis is a rhetorical device in which a sentence is deliberately left unfinished. The sentence usually ends in an ellipsis as in the first and last examples given below.

If I get hold of you I'll . . . !

His behaviour was – well I would rather not go there.

King Lear: I shall have revenges on you both
That all the world shall – I will do such things –
What they are yet, I know not, but they shall be
The terrors of the earth!

("King Lear" by William Shakespeare)

"If you lay a hand on her I'll . . . !"

Appositive

An appositive is a grammatical or rhetorical device in which a noun phrase, a noun, or series of nouns is placed beside a noun about which it is giving additional information.

Examples:

My student, Howard Jones, was becoming increasingly proficient at public speaking.

Sandy and Jane, both friends of mine, will be coming to the picnic.

No one, not even a single person, should have to endure that kind of abuse.

The dog, a Maremma called Danté, took care of the ostrich chicks.

Apophasis

Apophasis, (also called paralipsis, praeteritio or occupation), is a rhetorical device in which the speaker brings up a subject by denying that it should be brought up. The device is commonly used in political speeches. The device is can be used to distance the speaker from unfair claims whilst still bringing them up.

Examples:

I don't even want to talk about the allegation that my opponent made claims for funds he was not entitled to.

We won't discuss his previous misdemeanours.

I shall ignore the fact that Smith is a drunk and a gambler who beats his wife, because we don't want personal issues to be a part of our discussion here.

Assonance

Assonance occurs when several words close to each other repeat the same vowel sound, but start with different consonants.

Examples:

He was tired and lied about being fired.

You will find assonance in the last three lines below from William Wordsworth's poem "Daffodils"

"I wandered lonely as a cloud
That floats on high o'er vales and hills'
When all at once I saw a crowd,
A host, of golden daffodils;
Beside the lake, beneath the trees,
Fluttering and dancing in the breeze . . ."

So, it's time to go and mow the lawn.

Asyndeton

Asyndeton is a rhetorical device in which conjunctions are omitted from a series of clauses thus making the statement stronger and more memorable.

The device is much more common in spoken English than it is in written English. When the device is used with appropriate tone, loudness and pauses, it can be very effective.

Examples:

A well-known example is, "I came, I saw, I conquered". (translated from the Latin, "Veni, vidi, vici." Julius Caesar)

In "Rhetoric" by Aristotle

"This is the villain among you who deceived you, who cheated you, who meant to betray you completely . . ."
"Let's take a look at the side. It's really thin. It's thinner than any smart phone out there, at 11.6 millimetres. Thinner than the Q, thinner than the Blackjack, thinner than all of them. It's really nice".
(Steve Jobs, 2007 Keynote Address)

"An empty stream, a great silence, an impenetrable forest. The air was thick, warm, heavy, sluggish, . . ."
("Heart of Darkness" by Joseph Conrad)

"We shall go on to the end, we shall fight in France, we shall fight on the seas and oceans, we shall fight with growing confidence . . ."
(Winston Churchill)

The unemployed were given caring, self-respect, training, jobs . . .!

Reduce, Reuse, Recycle.

Watch, Absorb, Understand.

Hardly breathing, pale and still, totally exhausted.

Bdelygmia

A rhetorical device derived from the Greek word meaning "filth" used to express hatred through a series of criticisms. The device is used to get the emotions of the audience, in this case hatred, in sync with the emotions of the speaker.

Bdelygmia is a type of hyperbole, and the extreme exaggerations are often a little "tongue in cheek".

Examples:

"A custom loathsome to the eye, hateful to the nose, harmful to the brain, dangerous to the lungs, and in the black, stinking fume thereof, nearest resembling the Stygian smoke of the pit that is bottomless".
(King James 1, 1604, "Counterblast to Tobacco")

"Well, I've got a staff meeting to go to and so do you, you elitist, Harvard, fascist, missed-the-dean's-list-two-semesters-in-a-row Yankee jackass".
(Allison Janney as C.J. Cregg in "The West Wing")

"Cigarettes are a filthy, horrible, disgusting habit. They pollute the air and poison children. Their purveyors are evil, wicked and mendacious promoters of death."
(changingminds.org – Use of language)

Bomphiolgia

A rhetorical device in which the speaker is involved in bombastic speech and exaggerates in a self-aggrandising manner. If you want to use this technique, try writing as many appropriate words that you can think of, and then use a thesaurus to get others.

Example:

I am the love of your life, the stars in your sky, your hero, your handsome partner. You could not possibly ask for anything else!

Brachyology

Brachyology is the removal of words that are not necessary for the core meaning being expressed. Sentences or phrases are condensed making the expression stronger.

Examples:

Love, hope, charity.

Me? (Is what you have for me?)

"Morning!" (for "good morning")

Cacophony

Cacophony is a mixture of harsh sounds.

Cacophony is used as a tool describing discordant situations with discordant words.

Examples:

"We want no parlay with you and your grisly gang who work your wicked will . . ."
(Winston Churchill)

"And being no stranger to the art of was, I have him a description of cannons, culverins, muskets, carabines, pistols, bullets, powder, swords, bayonets, battles, sieges, retreats, attacks, undermines, countermines, bombardments, sea-fights . . ."
(Jonathan Swift's "Gulliver's Travels")

"However, as they had left their cars blocking the road, a harsh, discordant din from those in the rear had been audible for some time, and added to the already violent confusion of the scene".
("The Great Gatsby" by F. Scott Fitzgerald, 1925)

Catachresis

In catachresis words or phrases are used in a way which is very different from their traditional usage. The word comes from the Greek word for "abuse", and the term originally meant abuse or misuse of grammar.

Examples:

After noticing the high price, his wallet could not be found.

To take arms against a sea of troubles.

"'Tis deepest winter in Lord Timon's purse".
(Shakespeare – "Timon of Athens")

"Blind mouths!"
(Milton – "Lycidas")

Chiasmus

In chiasmus two clauses are reversed and therefore balanced against each other.

Examples:

"Bad men live that they may eat and drink, whereas good men eat and drink that they may live".
(Socrates)

"I had a teacher I liked who used to say good fiction's job was to comfort the disturbed and disturb the comfortable".
(David Foster Wallace)

"Fair is foul, and foul is fair".
(Wiliam Shakespeare in "Macbeth")

Cliché

We associate clichés with sayings or phrases which are overused. The word comes from the French language and was originally used for a printing plate in which the cast letters were used over and over.

The use of clichés in speeches or presentation may have some use, but generally would be best avoided.

Examples:

As old as the hills.
Time will tell.
At the speed of light.
Scared out of my wits.
Frightened to death.
Every cloud has a silver lining.
What goes around comes around.
Fall head over heels.

Don't get your knickers in a knot.
Do you think I'm made of money.

Commoratio

Commoratio is repeating the same point over and over using different words.

The word comes from Latin and means to dwell on a point.

Examples:

"This parrot is no more. It has ceased to be. It's expired and gone to see its maker! This is a late parrot. It's a stiff! Bereft of life! It rests in peace! If you hadn't nailed it to the perch it would be pushing up daisies! It's run down the curtain and joined the choir invisible! This is an ex-parrot!"
(Monty Python – "The Dead Parrot Sketch")

"He's gone off his rocker!" shouted one of the fathers, aghast, and the other parents joined in the chorus of frightened shouting.
"He's crazy!" they shouted.
"He's nutty!"
"He's screwy!"
"He's batty!"
"He's dippy!"
"He's dotty!"
"He's daffy!"
"He's goofy!"
"He's buggy!"
"He's wacky!"
"He's loony!"
(Roald Dahl in "Charlie and the Chocolate Factory")

Conduplicatio

Conduplicatio is a rhetorical device in which one or more words are repeated in successive clauses. The purpose of conduplicatio is normally to amplify an idea.

Examples:

"Where have all the flowers gone?
Long time passing.
Where have all the flowers gone?
Long time ago.
Where have all the flowers gone?
Girls have picked them every one.
When will they ever learn?
When will they ever learn?"
(Pete Seeger and Joe Henderson, "Where Have All the Flowers Gone?")

"Fear leads to anger, Anger leads to hate. Hate leads to suffering."
(Yoda – "Star Wars")

"Blessed are the poor in spirit: for theirs is the kingdom of heaven.
Blessed are they that mourn: for they shall be comforted.
Blessed are the meek: for they shall inherit the earth.
Blessed are they that hunger and thirst after righteousness: for they shall be filled.
Blessed are the merciful: for they shall obtain mercy.
Blessed are the pure in heart: for they shall see God.
Blessed are the peacemakers: for they shall be called the sons of God.
Blessed are they that have been persecuted for righteousness' sake: for theirs is the kingdom of heaven."
(Jesus, Sermon on the Mount – Matthew 5:3-10)

Dehortatio

Dehortatio is a rhetorical device used to dissuade the audience from taking certain actions. The sentences using dehortio generally begin with "never" or "do not".

Examples:

Never look a gift horse in the mouth.

"Never give in, Never give in. Never, never, never, never --- in nothing, great or small, large or pretty --- never give in . . .".
(Winston Churchill)

"Never let a fool kiss you - - or a kiss fool you".
("Never Let a Fool Kiss You or a Kiss Fool You" – Viking 1999)

Distinctio

Distinctio is a literary device in which reference is made to multiple meanings of a word with the purpose of emphasising your intended meaning.

Examples:

When I said she was hot, I wasn't talking about the temperature, I meant that she was incredibly sexy.

Enthymeme

A term used to describe an incomplete argument.

Examples:

The defendant's fingerprints are on the weapon. So he must be guilty.

Epanalepsis

An epanalepsis is a literary device in which the initial word or words at the beginning of a sentence are repeated at its end also.

Examples:

The king is dead; long live the king.

"Blow winds and crack your cheeks! Rage blow!"
(William Shakespeare – "King Lear")

"A lie begets a lie."
(English proverb)

"Always Low Prices. Always"
(Advertising slogan)

"A minimum wage that is not a livable wage can never be a minimum wage".
(Ralph Nader)

Epieuxis

Epieuxis is a literary device in which there is repetition of a word or phrase to give it emphasis. There are usually no words in between.

Examples:

Location, Location, Location
(commonly used in real estate advertising)

"The horror, the horror"
(Joseph Conrad in "Heart of Darkness")

"Words, words, words."
("Hamlet" – William Shakespeare)

"Education, education, education"
(Tony Blair)

"It's a twister! It's a twister!"
(Zeke in "The Wizard of Oz" – 1939)

"Alone, alone, all, all alone
Alone on a wide, wide sea"
("The Rime of the Ancient Mariner" by Samuel Coleridge)

Epistrophe

Epistrophe which is also known as epiphora or antistrophe is the repetition of a word or words and the end of successive sentences or phrases. It tends to be a very emphatic device by placing the emphasis on the last word in a sentence or phrase.

Examples:

"When I was a child, I spoke as a child, I understood as a child, I thought as a child".
(Apostle Paul in the Bible – Cor 13:11)

"Who is here so base that would be a bondman? If any, speak; for him have I offended. Who is here so rude that would not be a Roman? If any, speak; for him have I offended. Who is here so vile that will not love his country? If any, speak; for him have I offended . . ."
(Brutus in "Julius Caesar" by William Shakespeare)

Epithet

An epithet is a word or a phrase used to describe a person or thing. It is often used instead of the actual name of the person or thing and thus becomes a type of nickname.

Examples:

Richard the Lionheart

Alexander the Great

Constantine the Great

Man's best friend (for a dog)

Ivan the Terrible

"The snotgreen sea. The scrotumtightening sea."
(James Joyce – "Ulysses")

Eponym

An eponym is a word based on a person's name or it can be a person, real or imaginary, from whom something else takes its name.

Examples:

Parkinsons disease

Hansens disease

Achilles' heel

Adam's apple

Alzeimer's disease

Asperger syndrome

Confucianism

Freudian slip

Exemplum

An exemplum is a real or imagined anecdote used to illustrate a point.

Examples:

Proverbs are examples of exempla (plural of exemplum)
Exempla were frequently used in medieval sermons.
Many have accomplished this skill, you can also.

Hendiadys

Hendiadys uses two words linked by the conjunction "and" to give emphasis.

Examples:

He was looking with his eyes and envy. (He was looking with envious eyes)

In spite of the weather and storm she still went to the function. (In spite of the stormy weather she still went to the function)

The girl sitting in front of the fireplace was nice and warm. (The girl sitting in front of the fireplace was nicely warm.)

Other words frequently joined by "and" include:

Sick and tired

Big and fat

Hyperbaton

In hyperbaton, words which naturally belong together are separated from each other to give greater emphasis.

Examples:

"Object there was none. Passion there was none".
(Edgar Allan Poe – "The Tell-Tale Heart")

"This is the sort of English up with which I will not put".
(Winston Churchill)

"The helmsman steered, the ship moved on; . . . Yet never a breeze up blew".
(Samuel Taylor Coleridge – "The Rime of the Ancient Mariner")

Hyperbole

Hyperbole is the use of extreme exaggeration to create a strong impression. Because of the gross exaggeration used in hyperbole it is not intended to be taken seriously. It is a very common element of Australian slang and numerous examples are given in my publication, "Aussie Humour and Slang" ISBN 13:978-1478207054.

Examples:

I have told you that a thousand times.

Her bag weighed a ton.

I would give anything for a cold beer.

I have a million things that I have to do.

I'm so hungry I could eat a horse

He's as old as the hills.

Below are a few examples from "Aussie Humour and Slang" by Ian McKenzie

The weather has been as dry as a dead dingo's donger.

She couldn't find a Grand Piano in a one roomed house.

He couldn't find a root in a brothel.

Hypophora

Hypophora is a rhetorical device in which the speaker poses a question to the audience, but then proceeds to answer it.

Examples:

"Do you know the difference between education and experience? Education is when you read the fine print; experience is when you don't".
(Pete Seeger in "Loose Talk' BY Linda Botts – 1980)

"You ask what is our aim? I can answer that in one word: It is victory, victory at all costs, victory in spite of all terror, victory, however long and hard the road may be".
(Winston Churchill – 1940)

Hypotaxis

Hypotaxis is a rhetorical device which arranges phrases or clauses into a subordinate relationship.

Examples:

"So sang a little Clod of Clay, Trodden with the cattle's feet".

("The Clod and the Pebble" by William Blake)

I was hungry, so I ate.

When I am alone, I feel lonely.

Hysteron-proteron

A hysteron-proteron is a literary device in which the normal order of terms are reversed. Putting the "cart" before the "horse".

Examples:

"I'm going to kill that magician. I'll dismember him and then I'll sue him".
(Woody Allen in "Oedipus Wrecks" in New Yoyk Stories – 1989)

Put on your shoes and socks.

Irony

Irony is the use of language which has an opposite meaning. It can be used for humour or empathy.

Examples:

It's ironic that the slang term for redheads in Australia is bluey.

The man who was grossly obese had the nickname of slim.

"How nice!" she said, I have to work and can't go to the concert.

"Water, water everywhere,
And all the boards did shrink;
Water, water everywhere,
Nor any drop to drink."
(Samuel Taylor Coleridge – "The Rime of the Ancient Mariner")

Litotes

Litotes is a deliberate form of understatement. The effect causes emphasis

Examples:

One example I give in my book, "Aussie Humour and Slang" is, "Bradman could play cricket a bit". (Sir Donald Bradman was a brilliant cricketer.)

Another example could be in referring to a woman who was very attractive. We might say, "she was not unattractive".

She is no oil painting. (She is ugly.)

This is no small problem. (This is a big problem.)

This wine is not bad at all. (This wine is very good.)

I am not as young as I used to be. (I am getting old.)

"The grave's a fine a private place,
But none, I think, do there embrace."

(Andrew Marvel - "To His Coy Mistress")

Metabasis

Metabasis is the transitioning from one subject to another. The word comes from the Latin and it means "a change". It is also claimed that the word comes from ancient Greek "Metábasis" meaning "changing mutation". The word is also used in medicine for a change in symptoms of a disease.

Examples:

You have heard lots of talk of what can go wrong with the plan, let's talk now about how it can succeed.

Methaphor

A metaphor is a commonly used rhetorical device used by speakers and in writing. Methaphors describe things that are not similar by asserting that in some way they are. It should not be confused with a simile which will use words such as "like" or "as" in making comparisons.

Examples:

A well-known metaphor is the one used by William Shakespeare in his play, "As You Like It".
"All the world's a stage,
And all the men and women are merely players;
They have their exits and their entrances;"

Some common metaphors include the following:

Broken heart

It's raining men
The light of my life
The apple of my eye
Feeling blue
Emotions are on a rollercoaster
He is the black sheep of the family
Hearing her friend was not injured was music to her ears
He was hopping mad
She was drowning in paperwork

William Shakespeare commonly used metaphors in his writing.
"Shall I compare Thee to a summer's Day". ("Sonnet 18")

Metonymy

Metonymy is the use of a word or a phrase which is different from what is being described, but has some association with it.

Examples:

Hollywood is a suburb of Los Angeles in California, U.S.A.. But the word "Hollywood" is often used as a metonym for the U.S. film industry.

The term "Buckingham Palace" is also sometime used metonymously to refer to the British royalty.

The financial centre of the U.S.A. is often referred to as "Wall Street".

"The pen is mightier than the sword".
(Written word is more important than force.)

"The White House will be making a decision today".

"The library was a help to the students".

"Give me a hand to finish these tasks please".

Onomatopoeia

Onomatopoeia uses words which phonetically sound like the sound they are being used to describe. Onomatopoeia can be a powerful tool for both speakers and writers, as it allows the audience to have some emotional involvement with the words being used.

Examples:

a-ha	jingle	wow
ah-choo	kerplunk	
bam	meow	
bash	moo	
bingle	mumble	
boom	murmur	
clang	neigh	
clank	oink	
clap	purr	
clatter	quack	
click	ribbit	
clink	screech	
cluck	slap	
cock-a-doodle-doo	splash	
cough	spray	
cuckoo	sprinkle	
ding	squirt	
drip	swish	
drizzle	swoosh	
flutter	thud	
gasp	thump	
giggle	tweet	
growl	warble	
grunt	whiff	
gurgle	whip	
gush	whisper	
hiss	whizz	
	whoosh	

Oxymoron

An oxymoron is a literary device in which seemingly contradictory elements appear side by side.

Examples:

Living dead
Cruel kindness
Making haste slowly
Alone together
Bitter sweet
Awfully good
Deafening silence
Deceptively honest
Good grief
Lead balloon
Plastic glasses
Pretty ugly
Unbiased opinion

Parallelism

Parallelism is a rhetorical device in which parts of sentences are given a similar form, thus giving a definite pattern.

Examples:

Easy come, easy go.
Like father, like son.
What goes around comes around.
"To err is human, to forgive divine." (Alexander Pope)
"I don't want to live on in my work. I want to live on in my apartment." (Woody Allen)

Paronomasia

Paronomasia is also known as a pun. It is a device in which a word is used in different senses or words with similar sounds are used to achieve a desired effect, often dual meaning.

Examples:

"Well, I'd rather have a bottle in front of me than a frontal lobotomy".
(Tom Waits in "fernwood2Night", 1977)

"Contraceptives should be used on every conceivable occasion".
(Spike Milligan)

Drilling for oil is boring.

I do it for the pun of it.

The perfume was worth every scent it cost.

Without geometry, life is pointless.

Why is it easy for hunters to find leopards? Because leopards are always spotted.

I work as a baker because I knead the dough.

I gave my masseur the sack. He rubbed me up the wrong way.

Photographers never die, they just stop developing.

The difference between a conductor and a teacher is, the conductor minds the train and the teacher trains the mind.

Personification

Personification is the attribution of human qualities to animals or to things which are inanimate.

Examples:

Time and tide waits for none.

Opportunity was knocking at his door.

The parched earth was begging for water.

"We never sleep". (Sign outside a shop)

Kiss your integrity goodbye.

Pleonasm

Pleonasm is the use of more words than are needed to give a clear meaning.

Examples:

Burning fire
Free gift
First ever inaugural event
True fact
Tiny, small child
Absolutely necessary
Advance planning
Affirmative yes
Artificial prosthesis
Collaborate together
Completely destroyed
Eradicate completely

Filled to capacity
Minestrone soup
Old proverb
Pair of twins
Please RSVP

Polypoton

Polypoton is a rhetorical device in which words derived from the same root are repeated but giving a different sense.

Examples:

Power corrupts, but absolute power corrupts absolutely.

Love is an irresistible desire to be irresistibly desired.

Polysynditon

Polysynditon is the use of several conjunctions in succession.

Examples:

"Its got awesome security. And the right apps. Its got everything from Cocoa and the graphics and its got core animation built in and its got the audio and videl that OSX is famous for. Its got all the stuff we want".
(Steve Jobs – Macworld Keynote Address – 2007)

"Mrs. Hurst and her sister allowed it to be so – but still they admired her and liked her, and pronounced her to be a sweet girl, and one whom they would not object to know more of".
(Jane Austin – "Pride and Prejudice")

Rhetorical Question

A rhetorical is a question asked that does not require an answer. It is used to make a point, and is a commonly used rhetorical device in speeches.

Examples:

"Here was a Caesar! When comes such another?"
(Mark Anthony in "Julius Caesar" Act 3, scene 2)

"How do you solve a problem like Maria?"
(Rodgers and Hammerstein musical – "The Sound of Music")

"Marriage is a wonderful institution, but who would want to live in an institution?"
(H. L. Mencken)

"Isn't it a bit unnerving that doctors call what they do "practice'?"
(George Carlin)

Who knows?

Why not?

Is this supposed to be some kind of joke?

Is the Pope a catholic?

But who's counting?

This is hopeless, isn't it?

There is no point, is there?

Can fish swim?

Why bother?

Scesis Onomaton

This is a rhetorical device in which the speaker uses several different words which have the same or very similar meaning in order to emphasise a point.

Examples:

"The Dead Parrot" sketch from "Monty Python" has already been mentioned. But, it is one of my favourites and is a great example of scesis onomaton.

"It's not pining; it's passed on! This parrot is no more! It has ceased to be! It's expired and gone to meet its maker! This is a late parrot! It's a stiff! Bereft of life! It rests in peace! If you hadn't nailed it to the perch, it would be pushing up the daisies! It's run down the curtain and joined the choir invisible! This is an ex-parrot!"

Sentenial Adverb

A sentenial adverb is a word or phrase which gives emphasis to the words immediately proximate to the adverb.

Examples:

You are quite right.

She was very late.

Any of the following included in a sentence will be sentenial adverbs
    In fact
    Of course
    Without doubt

In short
Assuredly
Certainly

Simile

A simile is a rhetorical device used both orally and in writing where a comparison is made between two different things. The words "like" or "as" are commonly used in similes.

Some similes include:

As black as coal
As blind as a bat
The dam was as dry as a bone
He is as cunning as a fox
As cute as a kitten
As snug as a bug in a rug
As bold as brass
As bright as a button
As busy as a bee
As clear as a bell
As cool as a cucumber
As light as a feather
As plain as day
As sharp as a razor

Many similes such as the ones listed above are very well known and should therefore be used with caution. You may by using them be accused of using clichés. Over use of clichés can be indicative of a lack of original thought.

Syllepsis

Syllepsis is a rhetorical device in which one word simultaneously modifies two or more other words, but each modification needs to be understood differently.

Examples:

He arrived late and in his Mercedes.
She lowered her standards by raising her glass, her courage, her eyes and his hopes. (Flanders and Swann)
The winemaker prefers pressing grapes to clothes.

Symploce

Symploce is the combination of anaphora and epistrophe. It involves the repetition of words or phrases at both the beginning and the end of successive clauses.

Examples:

"For want of a nail the shoe was lost.
For want of a shoe the horse was lost.
For want of a horse the rider was lost.
For want of a rider the battle was lost.
For want of a battle the kingdom was lost.
And all for the want of a horseshoe nail."
(attributed to Benjamin Franklin)

Synathroesmus

Synathroesmus is the rhetorical device of piling up several terms together. They are usually adjectives and are used as an insult.

Examples:

I remember one example of synathroesmus from when I was quite young. "You flat footed, louse bound, floppy eared weasel . . ."

"He was a gasping, wheezing, clutching, covetous old man."
(Charles Dickens – "A Christmas Carol")

Synecdoche

Synecdoche is from the Greek language and means simultaneous understanding. It is a rhetorical device in which a part of something refers to its whole and vice versa.

Examples:

Hired hands (refers to hired workers)
The word "wheels" can refer to a whole vehicle.
A "breadwinner" is the person who earns money to purchase food etc.
The word "bread" can refer to both food and money.
At the Olympic Games you might hear of Australia winning a gold medal. The medal was won by an individual or a team from Australia.

Tapinosis

Tapinosis is a rhetorical device in which less importance is given to something than is really deserved.

Examples:

Your team didn't win, the other team lost.
"It's just a flesh wound." (Monty Python referring to an amputated leg)

Tricolon

I remember learning about tricolons in a subject called "Classical Rhetoric" which I studied as part of my undergraduate Arts degree back in the 1970's. It is a very commonly used rhetorical device which has been used by great orators throughout history.

A true tricolon has three verbs of equal length. So, the Latin version of Julius Caesar's quote below is a true tricolon. The English version is not.

Regardless of whether it is a true tricolon or not, having a list of three words, phrases, or clauses is a very powerful rhetorical device. For some reason, the number three has much more power than two or four or any other number. Orators have been aware of this throughout history.

Examples:

A well known of tricolon is in Julius Caesar. "Veni, vidi, vici." ("I came, I saw, I conquered")

"Tell me and I forget. Teach me and I remember. Involve me and I learn."
(Benjamin Franklin)

"Be sincere, be brief, be seated."
(Franklin D. Roosevelt's advice to speakers)

"I require three things in a man. He must be handsome, ruthless and stupid."
(Dorothy Parker)

"Friends, Romans, Countrymen . . ."
(Brutus's speech in Julius Caesar)

The good, the bad, and the ugly.

"Father, Son and Holy Spirit"
(Bible)

The truth, the whole truth, and nothing but the truth.

Location, location, location
(common real estate promotion)

Understatement

An understatement is a form of speech in which far less importance is given to someone or something than should be given.

Examples:

Bradman could play cricket a bit.

"Our opinions may differ slightly on how we should handle this." (When the opinions are very different)

"I know a little about tax law." (Statement from a prominent taxation lawyer)

"She is not such a bad looking girl." (referring to a beautiful woman)

"That could have been handled better."(Talking to someone who really stuffed something up)

Zeugma

Zeugma is a rhetorical device in which a word can apply to different parts of a sentence giving different meanings.

Examples:

"You are free to execute your laws and your citizens, as you see fit."
(Star Wars)

Postscript

With just a few minor changes, this book "Useful Rhetorical Devices" is a copy of chapter 11 of my book, "Powerful, Professional, Personal Presentations". The ISBN of the paperback version is 978-14848125787. As rhetorical devices are useful tools for both writers and orators, it was decided to produce this mini book as an additional publication.

Any book on business or communication that I publish as a paperback, I also make available as inexpensive e-books which are available via instant download. You can find the e-book versions at Google Play, iTunes, Amazon Kindle, Nook Books and all major e-book sellers.

To find other titles and various distributors, go to:

www.iansbooks.com

Ian McKenzie

Made in the USA
Monee, IL
23 September 2024

66388068R00035